What It Takes to Stage a Play

by Leah Johnson

Scott Foresman
is an imprint of

PEARSON

Glenview, Illinois • Boston, Massachusetts • Mesa, Arizona
Shoreview, Minnesota • Upper Saddle River, New Jersey

ISBN 13: 978-0-328-39480-7
ISBN 10:   0-328-39480-7

If you've ever seen a play, you know that at the end of the play, you clap for the actors. Their performance is entertaining. But they are just one part of the performance. Many people work together for many hours to put on a play. Without teamwork, a play could not go on. You see the actors on stage, but there are many other people who work behind the scenes. Do you know what they do? Let's go backstage and find out!

The actors take a bow at the end of the show.

Costumes help transform the actors into their characters.

The people who work behind the scenes of a play are called the "crew." Some crew members control the show's lighting. The costume crew designs and sews the costumes. The props crew finds the "props," or things that the actors will touch, hold, or use during the play.

The costumes are an important part of the play. They help make the characters in the play look real. Some costumes look like everyday clothes. Other costumes are fancy. Plays about kings and queens need costumes that will transform the actor into a **descendant** of a royal family.

**The costumes often begin as drawings
made by the technical director.**

The technical director is in charge of the set,
or scenery. He or she designs the set for each
scene in the play. The technical director's crew
builds and paints the set. He or she also designs
the costumes and decides how lights will be used.
The technical director gives his crew **advice** on
how to make the stage look its best for the play.

Set builders are busy backstage.

Backstage there is the buzz of activity. *Clap! Bang! Buzz!* The crew is building the sets. Builders hammer, saw, and sand pieces of wood. Some of the wooden frames are covered with cloth to make "flats." Other crew members paint the flats to make them look like clouds, buildings, and other backgrounds. The painted flats will look real from the seats in the audience!

Much of the stage manager's job is to control the special effects on stage.

Every play needs a stage manager. The stage manager is the person who makes the show go smoothly. He or she has many jobs, such as making sure that the lights come on at the right time. The stage manager is also in charge of special effects like smoke and rain and sound effects like thunder. The stage manager tells the crew when to change the scenery or put props on the stage.

The director leads the actors and crew.

Of the dozens of people who work on the play, the person "in charge" is the director. This person knows everything about the play. The director has studied the script and knows how he or she wants to present the play to the audience.

Auditions are announced in newspapers and on the Internet.

The director chooses the actors, or cast, for the play. Nothing is more important than choosing the right actors to fill each role.

Actors must audition to win a role in the play.

The director makes **arrangements** to hold tryouts, or auditions at the theater. The director needs to cast the play. Many actors will audition, but not everyone will get a part. Auditions may go on for many days. Sometimes actors must come back to audition a second time. When the director decides who will have each part, a cast list is posted. The actors who find their name on the list will be in the play. The other actors will not.

Once the play has been cast, rehearsals begin.

The first rehearsal includes the entire cast and crew. The cast sits around a table to read the script aloud, while the people who work backstage listen. The director gives everyone a rehearsal schedule. The cast and crew will work together for several weeks to get ready for opening night.

Finally, rehearsals begin. This is an exciting time for everyone. The cast and crew must work as a team. While the actors practice onstage, everyone else puts the pieces of the play together backstage.

The director must be able to get along with everyone who works on the play. Sometimes the director has to settle **arguments** between people who work on the play.

All of a play's props and scenery must be purchased or built, and the play's program and posters must be paid for.

Another person behind the scenes is the business manager. All those props cost money! Lumber, cloth, and paint cost money too. The business manager takes care of these kinds of expenses and balances the budget. The business manager is trusted to carefully handle the play's money. There's no room for **dishonesty**.

The audience applauds to show their appreciation for the cast and crew.

Staging a play is hard work. The play usually runs into a **snag** or two. Costumes rip. Props break. Actors sometimes forget their lines. But the show must go on! A good cast and crew will not let a snag ruin the show. If everyone works together, even the worst problems can be solved.

The next time you see a play, remember to cheer for the people backstage too. Without them, the play would not have been possible.

Glossary

advice *n.* an opinion about what should be done; suggestion

arguments *n.* discussions by persons who disagree; disputes

arrangements *n.* adjustments, settlements, or agreements

descendant *n.* person born of a certain family or group

dishonesty *n.* lack of honesty

script *n.* manuscript of a play, movie, or radio or TV show

snag *n.* a hidden or unexpected obstacle